ACRONYMVILLE
YOUR
ONE STOP
DESTINATION
IN THE WORLD
OF ACRONYMS

ABOUT THE AUTHOR

John Ross Harvey

Website

http://stores.lulu.com/tfoe

Profile

I am an author in spirit and a draftsman in reality. My left hand can alter compasses. I hate bad drivers especially in grey cars, and the Ferrari F1 team. I firmly believe every word can be explained by several others, and that is why you are here! You can find my other books under my website link

Always remember that driving a Snow Impaired vehicle is a commitment of SINS. Find SINS on Facebook.

TABLE OF CONTENTS

ACTION

SOCCER

Scoring

Optional

Champions

Carouse

Everywhere

Regardless

- *Soccer*

PISS

Perhaps

Inebriation

Spills

Some

- *Piss*

FLAMING

Frequent

Losers

Accosting

Many

In

Nonsensical

Generalizations

- *Flaming*

HOLD

Having

Obvious

Limits

Determined

- *Hold*

<u>RECREATION</u>

Requiring

Extreme

Care

Regarding

Exertion

And

Trusting

Instructors

Observations

Necessary

- *Recreation*

ACCIDENT

Actually

Caused

Completely

In

Disastrous

Extremes

Needing

Training

- *Accident*

VOYEURISM

Vixens

Over

Yonder

Enticingly

Unbelievably

Revealing

Instantly

Satisfying

Men

- *Voyeurism*

FOCUS

Fairly

Obvious

Concentration

Usually

Suggested

- *Focus*

EYE

Everything

You

Experience

- *Eye*

MURDER

Mis-

Understood

Recluse

Desires

Executing

Recently

- *Murder*

SPEECH

Some

People

Exclaim

Enthusiastic

Conversation

Happily

- *Speech*

IMPAIRED

Its

Most

People

Actually,

If

Reduced

Eyesight

Determined

- *Impaired*

STUPID

Simple

Tasks

Underestimate

People's

Infinite

Dumbness

- *Stupid*

RECORD

Requiring

Electrical

Connections

Organizing

Raw

Data

- *Record*

MIMIC

Mostly

It's

Miming

Initial

Conversation

- *Mimic*

VERBATIM

Virtual

Expressed

Response

Becomes

Actually

The

Initial

Message

- *Verbatim*

SEND

Simply

Execute

Necessary

Delivery

- *Send*

LEAVE

Letting

Everyone

Actually

Venture

Elsewhere

- *Leave*

ANIMAL

ROOSTER

Regularly

Orating

Outspoken

Song

To

Everyone

Really

- *Rooster*

LAMBS

Little

Animals

Make

Blankets

Soft

- *Lambs*

BAT

Bloody

Avian

Thing

- *Bat*

SNAIL

Slowness

Not

Always

Its

Livelihood

- *Snail*

TURTLE

Terribly

Undersized

Reptile

Takes

Long

Excursions

- *Turtle*

CATS

Certainly

Are

Terrifying

Subjects

- *Cats*

FISH

Frolicking

In

Sea

Home

- *Fish*

BEAR

Blueberry

Eating

Alaskan

Resident

- *Bear*

SLUG

Slippery

Lazy

Ugly

Grub

- *Slug*

PIG

Porker

Ingests

Garbage

- *Pig*

LION

Lazy

Irrational

Overlord

Needed

- *Lion*

CROWS

Conceptually

Rodents

On

Wings

Supposedly

- *Crows*

SHEEP

Shaved

Horned

Eloper

Excites

Pervert

- *Sheep*

SEAL

Swims

Excitedly

After

Lunch

- *Seal*

ARCHITECTURE

ARCH

A

Rounded

Construct

Hopefully

- *Arch*

GARAGE

Generally

A

Regular

Area

Guys

Exist

- *Garage*

MUSEUM

Most

Unusual

Subjects

Enter

Ugly

Museums

- *Museum*

STAIR

Structure

To

Allow

In

Rising

- *Stair*

STORE

Specialist

Trade

Organization

Retail

Exchange

- *Store*

ARENA

Actually

Requires

Enormously

Needy

Audience

- *Arena*

TOWER

Top

Of

World

Engineering

Required

- *Tower*

LOFTS

Lovely

Old

Factories

Turned

Suburban

- *Lofts*

LIBRARY

Looking

In

Books,

Reading,

Avoid

Rowdy

Yelling!

- *Library*

BRIDGE

Basic

Requirement

In

Driving

Great

Expanse

- *Bridge*

CASINO

Cash

Accepted

Sufficiently

In

New

Orleans

- *Casino*

AUTOMOTIVE

HYBRID

Hydro

Yields

Better

Results

In

Driverseat

- *Hybrid*

SUV

Seriously

Ugly

Vehicles

- *SUV*

RIM

Round

Industrious

Magnesium

- *Rim*

GM

Get

Mechanic

- *GM*

MOBILE

Mostly

Objects

Barreling

Into

Large

Expressways

- *Mobile*

DEFROSTER

Doesn't

Eliminate (all)

Frost

Required (for)

Seeing

Through

Exterior

Really

- *Defroster*

WIPERS

Winter

Instrument

Potentially

Except

Requires

Scrapers

- *Wipers*

START

Special

Tarmac

At

Racing

Tracks

- *Start*

SIGNAL

Switch

Is

Generally

Needed

At

Light

- *Signal*

ASTON MARTIN

Any

Spy's

Toy

Only

Needs

Missiles

And

Rockets

To

Impart

Negotiation

- *Aston Martin*

TANK

Tanks

Actually

Need

Kills

- *Tank*

TOW

Trouble

On

Wheels

- *Tow*

TOYOTA

Totally

Obnoxious

Yanks

Own

These

Anyway

- *Toyota*

MAZDA

Most

Always

Zooming

Dangerously

Anyway

- *Mazda*

TRIUMPH

To

Race

I

Understand

Miles

Per

Hour

- *Triumph*

HONDA

How

Often

Nobody's

Driving

Actually

- *Honda*

AUDI

Accelerates

Under

Dangerous

Intentions

- *Audi*

DATSUN

Do

Any

Teens

Suddenly

Under appreciate

Nissans

- *Datsun*

ROAD

Route

Of

Anyone

Driving

- *Road*

MOTORIST

Most

Ordinary

Travelers

Otherwise

Risking

Individual

Safety

Totally

- *Motorist*

FIAT

Ferrari

Is

A

Toy

- *Fiat*

DRIVER

Drivers

Regularly

Inside

Vehicles

Expect

Respect

- *Driver*

ZAMBONI

Zooms

Around

Most

Boringly

On

New

Ice

- *Zamboni*

NISSAN

Not

Insured

Since

Sometime

After

November

- *Nissan*

BMW

Brain

Membranes

Went

- *BMW*

IMPALA

It

Must

Possess

All (6) (4 is a BelAir)

Lights

Always

- *Impala*

GAS

Guzzling

All

Savings

- *Gas*

PORSCHE

Pass

Or

Race

Slower

Cars

Here

Everyday

- *Porsche*

DODGE

Do

Only

Dads

Get

Excited

- *Dodge*

INFINITI

If

Nissan

Finished

Nice

Inside.

That's

It

- *Infiniti*

OLDSMOBILE

Only

Lazy

Dads

Seen

Motoring

On

Back roads

In

Luxurious

Excellence

- ***Oldsmobile***

VEHICLE

Vehicles

Essentially

Have

Individuals

Completely

Lacking

Experience

- *Vehicle*

PONTIAC

Passing

Only

Next

Truck

In

A

Convoy

- *Pontiac*

CHEVROLET

Crap

Heaps

Every

Vehicle

Rolls

Off

Line

Extremely

Terrible

- *Chevrolet*

GRID

Grid

Racecars

Immediately

Drivers

- *Grid*

TTC

Toronto's

Taxi

Companies

- *TTC*

CARS

Cars

Actually

Require

Skill

- *Cars*

BOY

ANDREW

Always

Needs

Direction

Regarding

Everything

West

- *Andrew*

RISTO

Reclusive

Introvert

Spends

Time

Observing

- *Risto*

STEPHEN

Sometimes

Tries

Extra

Potent

Hashish

Even

Now

- *Stephen*

LARRY

Lazy

And

Rarely

Remembers

You

- *Larry*

DAVE

Definitely

Always

Very

Excited

- *Dave*

KEITH

Killer

Entertainer

Is

Teen's

Heartthrob

- *Keith*

LUIGI

Lucky

Underling

Is

Genuinely

Intriguing

- *Luigi*

HARVEY

He's

Always

Right (on)

Virtually

Everything

Yes

- *Harvey*

FRED

Frequently

Requesting

Extra

Days

- *Fred*

JUSTIN

Just

Undergone

Surgery

To

Increase

Nose

- *Justin*

CALENDAR

WINTER

When

It's

Necessary

To

Escape

Reality

- *Winter*

SUMMER

Simply

Understood

Most

Men

Enjoy

Relaxation

- *Summer*

DECEMBER

Decidedly

Extreme

Cold

Expected

Making

Birds

Escape

Regularly

- *December*

APRIL

Any

Potential

Rain

Is

Late

- *April*

MARCH

Making

Any

Real

Canadians

Happy

- *March*

JUNE

June bugs

Usually

Not

Exterminated

- *June*

CELEBRITY

CARLIN (George)

Comedic

Argumentative

Rantman

Loved

Immensely

Now

- *Carlin (George) R.I.P.*

KING (Larry)

Killer

Interviewer

Never

Generalizes

- *King (Larry)*

PARTON (Dolly)

Possessing

Amazing

Red

Tights

Of

Nylon

- *Parton (Dolly)*

CYRUS (Miley)

Certainly

Young

Remains

Uber

Star

- *Cyrus (Miley)*

COOPER (Anderson)

Correspondent

Of

Other

People's

Eccentric

Recollections

- *Cooper (Anderson)*

SHATNER (William)

Simply

Has

Accosted

Trekkie

Nerds

Everywhere

Recently

- *Shatner (William)*

CRUZ (Penelope)

Cruise

Remembers

Undoing

Zippers

- *Cruz (Penelope)*

SPRINGER (Jerry)

Some

People

Remain

Incredibly

Neat

Giving

Incredible

Ratings

- *Springer (Jerry)*

AFLECK (Ben)

Actually

Found

Lopez

Extremely

Cute

Kissing

- *Afleck (Ben)*

STEWART (Jon)

Simply

Talks

Extremely

Weirdly

About

Republicans

Today

- *Stewart (Jon)*

WOODS (Tiger)

Wonder

Of

Ominous

Driving

Slices

- *Woods (Tiger)*

WEST (Kanye)

W.Bush

Eliminated

Spoken

Thoughts

- *West (Kanye)*

DEGENERES (Ellen)

Delightful

Eccentric

Genuine

Entertainer

Needs

Extremely

Real

Entertainment

Suggestions

- *Degeneres (Ellen)*

CROWE (Russell)

Certain

Reporters

Only

Wish

Exclusive

- *Crowe (Russell)*

AGUILERA (Christina)

A

Genuinely

Understood

Incredible

Lady

Expects

Records

Acknowledged

- *Aguilera (Christina)*

CYRUS (Billy Ray)

Career

Yelling

Remember

Us

Supposedly

- *Cyrus (Billy Ray)*

FOXWORTHY (Jeff)

Found

On

X-ray

Why

Only

Redneck

Tales

Happen

Yes?

- *Foxworthy (Jeff)*

DEPP (Johnny)

Definitely

Eccentric

Performing

Powerhouse

- *Depp (Johnny)*

KIDMAN (Nicole)

Keith

Is

Desired

Man

Actually

Now

- *Kidman (Nicole)*

ENGVALL (Bill)

Extremely

Nice

Guy

Verbalizing

About

Life's

Losers

- *Engvall (Bill)*

PACINO (Al)

Professional

Actor

Certainly

Is

Not

Ordinary

- *Pacino (Al)*

GORE (Al)

General

Of

Restoring

Environment

- *Gore (Al)*

STEWART (Patrick)

Some

Trekkers

Expect

Worf

And

Ryker

Too

- *Stewart (Patrick)*

SPEARS (Britney)

Some

Posters

Exhibited

At

Record

Stores

- *Spears (Britney)*

CRUISE (Tom)

Celebrity

Ritalin

User

Is

Scientology

Endorser

- *Cruise (Tom)*

FORD (Harrison)

Forgets

Only

Redheads

Daily

- *Ford (Harrison)*

LANE (Diane)

Looks

Amazing

Now

Even

- *Lane (Diane)*

VILLENEUVE (Jacques)

Very

Intelligent

Lazy

Looking

Einstein

Needing

Everyone

Understanding (His)

Vehicular

Excellence

- *Villeneuve (Jacques)*

WILLIS (Bruce)

What

I

Lack

Lately

Is

Sexiness

- *Willis (Bruce)*

REEVES (Keanu)

Regarding

Entertainment

Exploits

Virtually

Everything

Sucked

- *Reeves (Keanu)*

COLOUR

GOLD

Glitters

On

Loose

Dentures

- *Gold*

SILVER

Simply

Is

Lacking

Visual

Excitement

Really

- *Silver*

GREY

Generally

Regarded (with)

Extreme

Yawning

- *Grey*

PALE

Perhaps

A

Lighter

Example

- *Pale*

ORANGE

Opposing

Red

And

Not

Green

Either

- *Orange*

BLONDE

Brunette

Ladies

Only

Need

Dye

Essentially

- *Blonde*

AMBER

Actually

Makes

Braking

Early

Realistic

- *Amber*

PURPLE

Princes

Understand

Regal

Positions

Lack

Expression

- *Purple*

SALMON

Simply

Add

Little

More

Ordinary

Neutrals

- *Salmon*

BROWN

Butts

Regularly

Oust

Wondrous

Neutrals

- *Brown*

PINK

Paint

In

Nana's

Kitchen

- *Pink*

FUCHSIA

Fantastically

Underused

Colour

Homosexuals

Splatter

In

Apartments

- *Fuchsia*

GREEN

Gangrene

Retains

Exquisite

Examples

Naturally

- *Green*

BRUNETTE

Blondes,

Redheads,

Understand

Not

Everyone

Tames

Tresses

Equally

- *Brunette*

CONCEPT

BORED

Brilliant

Observations

Require

Extreme

Disassociation

- ***Bored***

HELP

Heroes

Essential (to)

Lazy

People

- ***Help***

SOME

Strictly

Observed

Matter

Essentially

- *Some*

LOVE

Lustily

Obsessing

Vixens

Eternally

- *Love*

CRIME

Cocaine

Runners

Ingest

Morphine

Eventually

- *Crime*

DRIVEN

Drivers

Required

In

Vehicles

Especially

Now

- *Driven*

ABOVE

Anti

Below

Or

Very

Elevated

- *Above*

BELOW

Bottom

Essentially

Last

Of

Whatever

- *Below*

DRY

Didn't

Rain

Yesterday

- *Dry*

VAGINA

Vitally

Aware

G-spot

Is

Needing

Arousal

- *Vagina*

SPERM

Semen

Projectiles

Expecting

Responses

Mostly

- *Sperm*

VEGAN

Virtually

Extinct

Genome

Around

Nebraska

- *Vegan*

LONG

Length

Only

Needs

Greatness

- *Long*

WIDE

Width

Is

Definitely

Enormous

- *Wide*

INTELLIGENCE

Its

Needed

To

Explain

Love,

Laughter,

Importance,

Generosity,

Economics,

Necessity,

Completely

Everything

- *Intelligence*

POETRY

Poets

Only

Express

Tales

Remarkably,

Yes?

- *Poetry*

FAIR

Frequently

An

Important

Response

- *Fair*

ONLY

One

Not

Lots

Yes

- *Only*

NUDE

No

Underwear

Definite

Exposure

- *Nude*

SALE

Selling

Anything

Leftover

Essentially

- *Sale*

MATH

Making

Algebra

Take

Hours

- *Math*

CHAOS

Cannot

Have

Anything

Obvious

Start

- *Chaos*

COMPOST

Certain

Organic

Materials

Piled

On

Some

Tarp

- *Compost*

MUST

Making

Understood

Some

Tasks

- *Must*

DATE

Definitely

A

Time

Expected

- *Date*

FINE

Frequently

Is

Not

Excellent

- *Fine*

SMELL

Simply

Makes

Everything

Linger

Longer

- *Smell*

MOST

Majority

Of

Some

Things

- *Most*

GARBAGE

Getting

Any

Refuse

Bagged

And

Gone

Essentially

- *Garbage*

OPTION

Only

Provide

To

Include

Other

Needs

- *Option*

MEMORY

Memorizing

Each

Moment

Of

Recent

Years

- *Memory*

ILL

Is

Legalized

Laziness

- *Ill*

TRIVIA

Total

Recall

In

Virtually

Insignificant

Arenas

- *Trivia*

GOOD

Greatness

Of

Other's

Deeds

- *Good*

RETRO

Respect

Everything

That's

Really

Old

- *Retro*

PLAN

Performing

Legal

Activities

Necessarily

- *Plan*

MY

Mostly

Yours

- *My*

FREE

Forget

Remuneration

Expect

Everything

- *Free*

FOOD & DRINK

SPICY

Sweet

Peppers

Induce

Crazy

Yelling

- *Spicy*

ALE

Anti

Lager

Essentially

- *Ale*

CARROT

Certainly

A

Rare

Root

Of

Taste

- *Carrot*

LAGER

Lacking

Ale's

Greatness

Economically

Realistic

- *Lager*

SWEET

Simply

Wonderfully

Excellent

Experienced

Taste

- *Sweet*

ROTI

Rastaman

Order

This

In

- *Roti*

GRAPES

Green

Ripe

And

Purple

Especially

Sweet

- *Grapes*

GOBLET

Great

Oversized

Bottled

Liquid's

Essential

Trinket

- *Goblet*

WATER

Wet

And

Tasteless

Essential

Refreshment

- *Water*

LATTE

Let's

Avoid

Tasting

The

Espresso

- *Latte*

BACON

Basically

A

Carnivore's

Only

Need

- *Bacon*

VODKA

Vladimirs

Often

Drink

Kremlin

Alcohol

- *Vodka*

FIBRE

Found

In

Bread,

Rolls, &

Excrement

- *Fibre*

ALCOHOL

All

Liquor

Certainly

Only

Has

Obvious

Limits

- *Alcohol*

BEER

Brewed

Extra

Essential

Refreshment

- *Beer*

HAM

How

About

Meat?

- *Ham*

PASTA

Penne

And

Spaghetti

Taste

Amazing

- *Pasta*

GARLIC

Good

And

Required

Lots

In

Cooking

- *Garlic*

BREAD

Butter

Required

Especially

After

Dentist

- ***Bread***

SUGAR

Some

Unhealthy

Granules

Are

Required

- ***Sugar***

STEAK

Such

Tender

Excellence,

Avoid

Ketchup

- *Steak*

FOOD

For

Our

Obligatory

Digestion

- *Food*

BEEF

Beautifully

Excellent

Essential

Food

- *Beef*

COFFEE

Coffee

Only

For

Fanatics

Especially

Espresso

- *Coffee*

ESPRESSO

Extremely

Strong

Product

Required (at)

Every

Secret

Society

Organization

- *Espresso*

TEA

Tea's

Excellent

Always

- *Tea*

GEOGRAPHY

ARCTIC

Actually

Really

Cold

To

Ice

Cubes

- *Arctic*

SITE

Somewhere

In

There

Essentially

- *Site*

NEVADA

Noticeably

Expensive

Visually

After

Dark

Always

- *Nevada*

BOSTON

Basically

Only

Small

Town

Of

New England

- *Boston*

AUSTRALIA

Amazingly

Underrated

Scenery

That

Real

Aboriginals

Live

In

Anyway

- *Australia*

PORT

Place

Of

Regular

Trade

- *Port*

DARFUR

Deadly

African

Revolution

Ferociously

Using

Ruthlessness

- *Darfur*

SWEDEN

Scandinavian

Wilderness

Excursions

Dodge

Elephants

Normally

- *Sweden*

TORONTO

Taxis

Or

Rickshaws

On

Next

Tour

Ordered

- *Toronto*

FINLAND

Families

In

Northern

Lapland

Are

Normally

Drunk

- *Finland*

BELGIUM

Brilliant

Eccentric

Lazy

Germans

In

Untaxed

Mansions

- *Belgium*

INDIA

Incredibly

Nice

Destination

In

Asia

- *India*

IRELAND

Incredibly

Remarkable

England's

Loss

And

Nature's

Design

- *Ireland*

WALES

What

Every

Lazy

Englishman

Seeks

- *Wales*

PORTUGAL

Please

Only

Relax

To

Undertake

Generous

Azurian

Luxury

- *Portugal*

IRAN

Innocent

Regarding

Any

Nukes

- *Iran*

JAPAN

Justifiably

All

Products

Are

New

- *Japan*

IRAQ

Innocent

Regarding

Al

Qaeda

- *Iraq*

CANADA

Certainly

Amazes

Now

A

Destiny

Awaits

- *Canada*

EGYPT

Everyone

Go

Yonder

Pyramid

Territory

- *Egypt*

<u>CHINA</u>

Canadians

Happy

It's

Not

Alaska

- *China*

GIRL

EMILY

Exciting

Minx

Is

Loving

You

- *Emily*

SARAH

Sexually

Arousing

Redhead's

Absolutely

Hot

- *Sarah*

LISA

Looks

Incredibly

Sexy

Anyway

- *Lisa*

TERESA

Taking

Everyone's

Requests

Even

Suggesting

Alternatives

- *Teresa*

CHRISTINA

Can

Hopefully

Remain

In

Skin

Tight

Infinitesimal

Negligees

Always

- *Christina*

EVA

Essentially

Very

Amazing

- *Eva*

NICOLE

Not

In

Cruise's

Official

Logbook

Ex-wife

- *Nicole*

LESLIE

Looks

Extremely

Sexy

Loitering

In

Entrance

- *Leslie*

PAMELA

Possibly

Altered

Mammories

Expect

Looks

Always

- *Pamela*

CLEAVAGE

Certain

Looks

Expected

Are

Voyeuristic

And

Generally

Enticing

- *Cleavage*

JULIE

Just

Underwent

Liposuction

In

Ecuador

- *Julie*

MARY

Mother

Augmenting

Religious

Youngling

- *Mary*

LINDA

Likely

In

No

Dress

Anyway

- *Linda*

SUE

She

Understands

Everything

- *Sue*

<u>RITA</u>

Religious

Italian

Trampy

Asexual

- *Rita*

<u>ROSA</u>

Rita's

Obnoxious

Sister

Always

- *Rosa*

GOVERNMENT

PUBLIC

Publicly

Under funded

Buildings

Lack

Intrinsic

Charm

- *Public*

CHENEY (Dick)

Can't

Have

Every

New

Executive

Yelling

- *Cheney (Dick)*

BIN LADEN (Osama)

Bearded

Individual

Not

Liking

American

Dynamite

Explosions

Nearby

- *Bin Laden (Osama)*

OBAMA (Barack)

Often

Barack

Articulates

Magic

Answers

- *Obama (Barack)*

CONSERVATIVES

Clearly

Oppressive

Nerdy

Suits

Expect

Raises

Via

Acquiring

Taxes

In

Virtually

Everything

Sold

- *Conservatives*

BUSH (George W.)

Barely

Understands

Simple

History

- *Bush (George W.)*

CIA

Criminally

Insane

Assassins

- *CIA*

NSA

National

Snooping

Association

- *NSA*

FBI

Frustrated

Bungling

Investigators

- *FBI*

MEDIA

ANIME

Animation

Needing

Immensely

Monstrous

Eyes

- *Anime*

DOLLAR

Disaster

Of

Low

Loonie

Actually

Recovered

- *Dollar*

CNN

Comedy

Not

News

- *CNN*

CABLE

Communication

And

Bandwidth

Lack

Excitement

- *Cable*

NBC

Not

Buying

Crap

- *NBC*

CBC

Cannot

Buy

Comedy

- *CBC*

CBS

Cancels

Bad

Shows

- *CBS*

CSI

Can't

Spell

It

- **CSI**

LOST

Look

Outstandingly

Superior

Television

- ***Lost (The show)***

PBS

Pretty

Boring

Shows

- ***PBS***

ABC

Already

Been

Cancelled

- ***ABC***

NEWS

New

Exclusive

Weird

Stuff

- *News*

MYTHOLOGY

LEPRECHAUNS

Little

Eccentric

People

Rarely

Ever

Create

Happiness

As

Usually

Never

Seen

- *Leprechauns*

ZEUS

Zeus

Expects

Unholy

Sex

- *Zeus*

ODIN

Only

Deity

In

Norway

- *Odin*

RA

Remarkably

Androgynous

- *Ra*

PEOPLE

BOOBS

Bosom

Observed

Objectively

Begs

Slobber

- *Boobs*

DIVA

Debutante

Is

Very

Arrogant

- *Diva*

SLUT

Single

Lady

Undresses

Totally

- *Slut*

PAGEANT

Parading

Amazing

Girls

Everywhere

And

Nobody

Talks

- *Pageant*

DUNCE

Definitely

Uninformed

Needing

Corrective

Education

- *Dunce*

LEG

Lovely

Enticing

Gams

- *Leg*

STRIPPER

Shredded

T-shirts

Removed

In

Passionate

Performance

Expects

Remuneration

- *Stripper*

SMART

Some

Mensas

Are

Really

Tremendous

- *Smart*

COUNCIL

Conversation

Of

Understood

Needs

Continues

In

Legislature

- *Council*

MAYOR

Mostly

Anyone

Yielding

Opposing

Reforms

- *Mayor*

MINISTER

Mostly

Is

Nice

In

Sermon

To

Everyone

Responding

- *Minister*

DUMB (the speechless meaning)

Don't

Underestimate

Mute

Beings

- *Dumb*

DEAF

Damaged

Ears

Are

Frustrating

- *Deaf*

CREATOR

Certain

Responsibility

Expected

About

Translating

Ordinary

Requirements

- *Creator*

PILOT

Plane

Is

Lifting

Off

Today

- *Pilot*

BRIGADE

Brutishly

Regimented

Infidels

Gather

Anybody

Desperately

Eccentric

- *Brigade*

ACID

Actually

Can

Inflame

Diaphragm

- *Acid*

CHILD

Certainly

Has

Its

Life's

Dramas

- *Child*

VILLIAN

Very

Inferior

Low

Life

Is

A

Nuisance

- *Villain*

BLOOD

Basic

Life

Of

Others

Desired

- *Blood*

PIRATE

Pillaging

Illegally

Required

And

Trade

Everything

- *Pirate*

DENTIST

Doesn't

Expect

Nice

Teeth

If

Suggesting

Toothpaste

- *Dentist*

ASSASSIN

Actually

Some

Sniper

Assessing

Simple

Shot

Is

Necessary

- ***Assassin***

NEANDERTHALS

No

Established

Aesthetics,

No

Daintiness,

Except

Rough

Thick

Hair

And

Long

Skulls

- *Neanderthals*

DARTH

Dead

Asthmatic

Rejuvenated

Through

Helmet

- *Darth*

PUNK

People

Underestimate

Nerdy

Kids

- *Punk*

LEADER

Lazy

Executive,

Annoying

Dictator

Expecting

Respect

- *Leader*

CHEF

Cooking

Horribly

Expensive

Food

- *Chef*

AUTHOR

Anyone's

Understood

Thoughts

Have

Obvious

Response

- *Author*

WITCH

Woman

Incinerated

To

Cheerful

Heckles

- *Witch*

FIGURES

Firstly

It's

Generally

Understood

Regular

Exercise

Sucks

- *Figures*

GUYS

Girls

Understand

You.

Sorry!

- *Guys*

GIRLS

Guys

Immediate

Reaction:

Looking

Sexy

- ***Girls***

GOD

Gracious

Omnipotent

Deity

- ***God***

HUMAN

How

Understanding

Man

Affects

Noone

- *Human*

BRIDE

Beauty

Radiates

In

Dutiful

Expectation

- *Bride*

SPACE

SUN

Star

Undeniably

Necessary

- *Sun*

SATURN

Someone

Actually

Thought

Up

Ring's

Need

- *Saturn*

COMET

Cold

Ominous

Meteor

Expected

Tentatively

- *Comet*

PLUTO

Planetary (Status)

Loss

Understood

To

Observatories

- *Pluto*

PLANET

People

Like

Assuming

No

Extra

Terrestrials

- *Planet*

MOON

Most

Others

Observe

Nightly

- *Moon*

STAR TREK

STAR TREK

Spock

Takes

A

Reading

Then

Responds

Exclusively (to)

Kirk

- *Star Trek*

BORG

Brilliantly

Organized

Robotic

Government

- *Borg*

McCOY (Bones)

Mostly

Cantankerous

Commander

Only

Yells

- *McCoy (Bones)*

CRUSHER (Beverly)

Carefully

Removes

Unsightly

Scars,

Health

Experience

Respected

- *Crusher (Beverly)*

<u>LaFORGE (Geordi)</u>

Looks

Amazingly

Focused

On

Repairing

Generic

Engineering

- *LaForge (Geordi)*

<u>DATA</u>

Diabolical

Android

That's

Alive!

- *Data*

VULCAN

Virtually

Understood

Logic

Can

Appear

Nasty

- *Vulcan*

PICARD

Potentially

Important

Captain

Actually

Requires

Data

- *Picard*

WORF

Whom

Officers

Respect

Fearfully

- *Worf*

ROMULAN

Rarely

Objective

Monsters

Understand

Logics

Aren't

Necessary

- *Romulan*

SPOCK

Specialist

Performing

Only

Common

Knowledge

- *Spock*

TEAM

CELTICS (BOSTON)

Certainly

Eradicated

Lakers

Taking

Its

Championship

Superbly

- *Celtics*

ARGOS

Actually

Really

Great

Offense

Supposedly

- *Argos*

BULLS (Chicago)

Brilliantly

Underrated

Long

Legged

Shooters

- *Bulls*

LEAFS

Losing

Every time

A

Fan's

Sick

- *Leafs*

HABS (Montreal Canadians)

Hockey

At

Bell Centre

Sucks

- *Habs (Montreal Canadiens)*

BILLS (Buffalo)

Buffalo

Is

Losing

Lots (of)

Superbowls

- *Bills (Buffalo)*

CUBS (Chicago)

Chicago's

Underappreciated

Baseball

Squad

- *Cubs (Chicago)*

RAPTORS

Remains

A

Pathetic

Team

Of

Rejected

Shooters

- *Raptors*

TECHNOLOGY

GREEN

Green

Requires

Engineering

Excellence

Now

- *Green*

I-POD

Is

Personally

Organized

Downloads

- *I-pod*

BATTERIES

Basic

Alkaline

Technology

To

Extend

Resources

In

Electronic

Systems

- ***Batteries***

MICROWAVE

Makes

It

Completely

Redundant

Only

When

Anything

Valuable

Explodes

- *Microwave*

MEDIA

Most

Electronic

Data

Is

Alterable

- *Media*

RADIO

Relaxing

Anyone

Dancing

In

Overalls

- *Radio*

PIPE

Positively

Important

Plumbing

Engineering

- *Pipe*

ELECTRICAL

Even

Lazy

Electricians

Can

Test

Regularly

In

Currents,

Amperages, (&)

Loads

- *Electrical*

OVEN

Overcooked

Venison

Expected

Nightly

- *Oven*

BEAM

Building

Engineering

Accommodates

Mass

- *Beam*

ELECTRONIC

Every

Little

Eccentric

Creation

Takes

Regular

Or

Ni-Cad (Batteries)

Inside

Contraption

- *Electronic*

DRAIN

Dripping

Rain

Actually

Invites

Need

- *Drain*

DISH

Disabled

If

Satellite

Hovers

- *Dish*

WATCH

What

Any

Time

Contraption

Has

- *Watch*

MACHINE

Making

A

Construct

Have

Its

Necessary

Engine

- *Machine*

TOOLS

Technically

Obvious

Objects

Look

Strange

- *Tools*

PHONE

People

Hate

Overly

Nice

Electronics

- *Phone*

CD

Corruptible

Data

- *CD*

DVD

Dick

Van

Dyke

- *DVD*

CODE

Complex

Order

Data

Essentially

- *Code*

AT&T

Attacking (with)

Telephones

Today

- *AT&T*

EMAIL

Exciting

Messages

About

Inducing

Laughter

- *Email*

SPAM

Spewed

Personally

Accosting

Messages

- *Spam*

DIGITAL

Digital

Information

Gives

Industry

Technological

Advantages

Lately

- *Digital*

THING

GASOLINE

Guzzling

Any

Savings

Of

Lesser

Enumerated

Nameless

Employees

- *Gasoline*

HERE

Having

Existence

Required

Essentially

- *Here*

BOARD

Built

Of

A

Rare

Deciduous

- *Board*

DICTATOR

Diabolical

Ingrate

Creates

Tension

And

Terrorizes

Others

Regularly

- *Dictator*

PSYCHOPATH

Pathetic

Simpleton

You

Challenged

Happily

Over

Pathetic

Ability

To

Hate

- *Psychopath*

CIGAR

Certainly

Is

Gross

And

Revolting

- *Cigar*

ACRONYM

Amazing

Collection

Required

Of

Names

Yearning

Meanings

- *Acronym*

ROOT CANAL

Removal

Of

Overdead

Tooth

Construction

And

Nerve

Alleviated

Lovingly

- ***Root Canal***

IMAGE

Is

Mostly

A

Generated

Expression

- ***Image***

POOL (Water)

Peaceful

Outdoor

Ominous

Liquid

- *Pool*

CIVIL

Community

Is

Very

Intense

Legally

- *Civil*

TOMB

Trap

Of

Many

Burials

- *Tomb*

CIGARETTE

Crude

Incredibly

Gross

Aromas

Remain

Extremely

Terrible

To

Everybody

- *Cigarette*

STONE

Seeing

Time

Of

Neanderthals

Easily

- *Stone*

THIGH

Tight

Hard

Impressive

Gams

Here

- *Thigh*

TUSH

Tender

Untanned

Skin

Here

- *Tush*

HEMP

Helping

Everyone

Make

Pot

- *Hemp*

TALL

Truthfully

Anyone

Long

Legged

- *Tall*

THUMB

The

Hand's

Useful

Major

Bone

- *Thumb*

DART

Definitely

Aerodynamic

Reaching

Target

- *Dart*

MUSTACHE

Mostly

Under

Some

Thing

Above

Chin,

Hairs

Essentially

- *Mustache*

TRAIN

Track

Running

Automated

Infrastructure

Need

- ***Train***

WEED

Wow

Ever

Excellent

Dude!

- ***Weed***

BEAVER

Bell's

Electronic

Avatars

Virtually

Everywhere

Recently

- *Beaver*

CURL (Hair)

Completely

Underestimating

Rounded

Locks

- *Curl*

FOG

Frequently

Obscuring

Ground

- *Fog*

DEW

Definitely

Extra

Wet

- *Dew*

FROST

Firstly

Requiring

Obvious

Scraping

Truthfully

- *Frost*

BALLOON

Basically

Average

Latex

Looks

Ominous

Only

Now

- *Balloon*

GRAM

Generic

Required

Absolute

Measurement

- *Gram*

COLLEGE

Contains

Only

Lovely

Ladies

Each

Gymnastics

Exposition

- *College*

BELT

Below

Extremely

Large

Tummy

- *Belt*

SHOE

Simply

Helping

Odour

Extinguishment

- *Shoe*

SWEATER

Sweet

Weathergirls

Expected

Apparel

To

Entertain

Recluses

- *Sweater*

CASE

Carry

All

Satchel

Essentially

- *Case*

SNOWBANKS

Snow

Not

Obvious

Window

Be

Aware

Needs

Krafty

Snowbrush

- *Snowbanks*

PANTS

Perhaps

A

Necessary

Thing

Sometimes

- ***Pants***

FLOOR

Found

Lumber

Or

Only

Rug

- ***Floor***

BLINDS

Blocks

Light

In

Non

Desirable

Scenarios

- *Blinds*

COMMA

Certainly

Only

Makes

Messages

Annoying

- *Comma*

PLUG

Power

Lead

Understands

Grounding

- *Plug*

SWITCH

Some

Wiring

Is

Training

Compact

Halogens

- *Switch*

FUND

Finances

Understandably

Need

Donations

- *Fund*

REPORT

Required

Essential

Papers

Only

Redeem

Tasks

- *Report*

BOTTLE

Basic

Object

To

Trap

Liquid

Essentially

- *Bottle*

SHELF

Something

Holding

Extra

Large

Fruits

- *Shelf*

MAIL

Making

Anything

Important

Lost

- *Mail*

SNOWMAN

Snow

Necessary

Otherwise

Water

Makes

All

Nasty

- *Snowman*

LINE

Length

Is

Neatly

Executed

- *Line*

SINS

Snow

Impairment's

Not

Safe

- *Sins*

GUIDE

Genuinely

Understood

Instructions

Deliver

Excellence

- *Guide*

TABLE

Technically

A

Board

Laterally

Elevated

- *Table*

DRESS

Daringly

Revealing

Effeminately

Soft

Skin

- *Dress*

MINISKIRT

Men

Instantly

Notice

Infinitesimal

Swath,

Kicking

It

Reveals

Tush

- *Miniskirt*

APRON

A

Patterned

Rag

Of

Nylon

- *Apron*

WARDROBE

Wooden

And

Robust

Dresser

Remains

Obvious

Bedroom

Essential

- *Wardrobe*

BIKINI

Bra

Is

Kind

If

Nearly

Invisible

- *Bikini*

THONG

Technically

Has

Only

Nylon

G-string

- *Thong*

TINSEL

Tree

Icicles

Not

So

Especially

Lingering

- *Tinsel*

GIFT

Generosity

Is

From

Thoughtfulness

- *Gift*

ENEMA

Every

Needle

Extracted (from)

My

Ass

- *Enema*

SIGN

Sometimes

It

Gets

Noticed

- *Sign*

BED

Boudoir

Expects

Drama

- *Bed*

SNOWBRUSH

Snow

Not

On

Windows

Brush

Remainder

Unbelievably

Simple

Huh?

- *Snowbrush*

STEP

Stair

To

Elevate

People

- *Step*

AWARD

Actually

Won

A

Rare

Deed

- *Award*

COIN

Cash

Of

Immediate

Necessity

- *Coin*

A COLD

A

Creation

Of

Lord (of)

Darkness

- *Cold*

MIGRAINE

Massive

Intense

General

Resonating

Aura

Is

Never

Excellent

- *Migraine*

BRUSH

Brushing

Ridiculously

Unwanted

Snow

Happily

- *Brush*

COMPASS

Contains

Ordinary

Magnet

Positive

At

South

Section

- *Compass*

SCRAPER

Scrape

Crystalline

Residue

Away

Please

Expect

Removal

- *Scraper*

FLOWERS

Fragrant

Lovely

Organism

Women

Essentially

Require

Soon

- *Flowers*

SAIL

Simply

An

Immense

Linen

- *Sail*

LIPS

Looks

Impressive

Painted

Smartly

- *Lips*

DASHBOARD

Decidedly

Accumulating

Sufficiently

Having

Bills,

Old spice

Aromas,

Rubbish, (&)

Dinner

- *Dashboard*

SOUL

Something

Obsessed (by)

Underworld

Lord

- *Soul*

BONE

Body's

Only

Necessary

Engineering

- *Bone*

TOBACCO

Triggers

Odious

Breath

And

Cancer

Cell

Outgrowths

- *Tobacco*

BODY

Built

On

DNA

Yes

- *Body*

BRA

Breast

Rounding

Aid

- *Bra*

GATE

Generally

At

The

Entrance

- *Gate*

WIRE

What

Importantly

Retains

Electricity

- *Wire*

DRUGS

Drug

Runners

Underrate

Getting

Stoned

- *Drugs*

DISC

Data

In

Simple

Confines

- *Disc*

NOSE

Needs

Only

Smells

Essentially

- *Nose*

OIL

Overlord's

Important

Liquid

- *Oil*

SHIT

Smells

Horribly

In

Toilet

- *Shit*

EAR

Essential

Auditory

Receptor

- *Ear*

FIRE

Frequently

Instigating

Real

Explosions

- *Fire*

PODIUMS

Performers

Only

Desire

Is

Understandably

Making

Stage

- *Podiums*

HOME

House

Of

Modest

Expectations

- *Home*

ROBOT

Remotely

Operated

Body

Of

Titanium

- *Robot*

PENIS

Positive

Erection

Necessary

In

Sex

- *Penis*

CANDLE

Can

At

Night

Deliver

Light

Easily

- *Candle*

DROID

Dimwit

Robot

Organism

Interpreting

Data

- *Droid*

SHAMPOO

Shiny

Hair

After

Massaging

Product

Over

Ourselves

- *Shampoo*

SIREN

Sounding

In

Response (to)

Emergent

Needs

- *Siren*

CAMERA

Captures

Any

Motion

Even

Removed

Apparel

- *Camera*

PDF

Printer

Diseased

File

- *PDF*

RESTAURANT

Requiring

Excellent

Service

To

Anyone

Using

Restrooms

And

Needing

Toilet

- ***Restaurant***

CAN

Cylindrical

And

Necessary

- ***Can***

TISSUE

To

Intricately

Steal

Snot

Usually

Expeditiously

- *Tissue*

DOOR

Direction

Of

Outright

Removal

- *Door*

STAMP

Sticky

Tab

About

Mailing

Post

- *Stamp*

BRAINS

Brilliance

Requires

Actual

Intelligence

Not

Stupidity

- *Brains*

CHIP

Colossally

Handy

In

Poker

- *Chip*

RING

Remarkable

Incredibly

Nice

Gems

- *Ring*

HOUSE

Home

Of

Unusually

Structured

Engineering

- *House*

PAINT

Perhaps

All

Instances

Need

Thinner

- *Paint*

MONEY

Millions

Only

Needed

Especially

Yours

- *Money*

TRADEMARK

WINDOWS

Works

If

Not

Destroyed

Or

Works

Slowly

- *Windows*

VISTA

Virtually

Impossible

System

Techies

Avoid

- *Vista*

AUTOCAD

Any

Understood

Technical

Operation

Can

Acquire

Drawings

- *AutoCAD*

BARNEY

Brontosaurian

Accommodating

Rather

Nerdy

Excitable

Youths

- *Barney*

NINTENDO

Now

Inventing

New

Toy

Electronics

Needing

Discs

Only

- *Nintendo*

SEGA

Simple

Entertaining

Game

Animations

- *Sega*

BARBIE

Boobs

And

Round

Butt

Is

Excellent

- ***Barbie***

HILTON

Hotel

Industry's

Luxury

Towers

Of

Note

- ***Hilton***

ELMO

Excitable

Little

Monster

Only

- *Elmo*

SURVIVOR

Some

Urban

Recluses

Venturing

Into

Visually

Oppressed

Regions

- *Survivor*

BERT

Basically

Ernie's

Roommate

Truthfully

- *Bert*

ERNIE

Eccentric

Recluse

Needs

Interesting

Entertainment

- *Ernie*

LYCOS

Letting

Yahoo

Continue

Our

Search

- *Lycos*

KELLOGG

Kitchens

Expect

Long

Lists

Of

Great

Goods

- *Kellogg*

SEARS

Simply

Expect

Appliances

Requiring

Servicing

- *Sears*

NABOB

Not (just)

Any

Beans

Optimum

Beans

- *Nabob*

KRAFT

Kitchens

Require

Amazing

Food

Today

- *Kraft*

E-BAY

Everything's

Buyable

Anyways

Yes

- *E-Bay*

NASA

Never

Above

Secret

Areas

- *NASA*

IKEA

Instantly

Kaput

Economical

Assemblies

- *Ikea*

MICROSOFT

Mostly

Incompetent

Computer

Representatives

Offering

Software

Of

Finished

Technologies

- *Microsoft*

SONIC

Speedy

Outrageous

Nearly

Infamous

Cartoon

- *Sonic*

WEBKINZ

What

Every

Brat

Knows

Is

Needing

Zebras

- *Webkinz*

ACKNOWLEDGEMENTS

Thanks to anybody that has ever wondered what words mean, and hopefully we were successful in providing at least one possible explanation by means of an acronym (acrostic for the more knowledgeable readers).

If anyone actually buys this book, we may be able to afford a big thick Rib steak on the BBQ complete with Montreal Steak Spices and Guiness Bulls-eye barbeque sauce.

Thanks to my crazy Swedish brother-in-law for his contributions towards making this book a reality. You can check his humour out here:

Risto Klint

Website

http://www.scudfish.com

Profile

I'm a tap dancing astronaut who enjoys bear taming and single malt Irish whiskey. My fears include bees, spoons and flying goats, but especially squirrels that are untrustworthy.

www.ingramcontent.com/pod-product-compliance
Lightning Source LLC
Chambersburg PA
CBHW061347280526

45784CB00001B/166